EASY PIANO

APR 2023

LENNON LEGEND
The very best of John Lennon

ISBN 978-1-4950-0382-0

HAL•LEONARD®
CORPORATION
7777 W. BLUEMOUND RD. P.O. BOX 13819 MILWAUKEE, WI 53213

In Australia Contact:
Hal Leonard Australia Pty. Ltd.
4 Lentara Court
Cheltenham, Victoria, 3192 Australia
Email: ausadmin@halleonard.com.au

3012707566 0261

Visit Hal Leonard Online at
www.halleonard.com

BEAUTIFUL BOY
(Darling Boy)

Words and Music by
JOHN LENNON

Close your eyes, __ go to sleep, __ say a

have no fear. lit - tle prayer. The mon - ster's gone. __ He's Ev - 'ry day, __ in

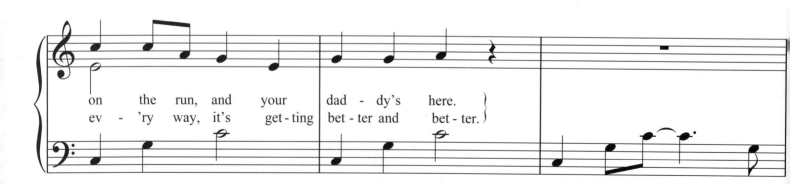

on the run, and your dad - dy's here. ev - 'ry way, it's get - ting bet - ter and bet - ter.

Beau - ti - ful, beau - ti - ful, beau - ti - ful, beau - ti - ful

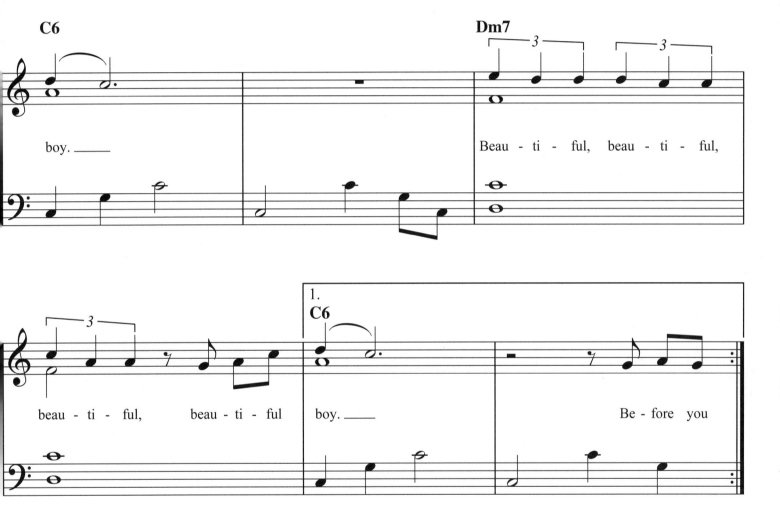

boy. _____

Beau - ti - ful, beau - ti - ful,

beau - ti - ful, beau - ti - ful boy. _____

Be - fore you

boy. _____

Out on the

Am(maj7)   **Am7**   **A**

o - cean,   sail - ing a - way, ___

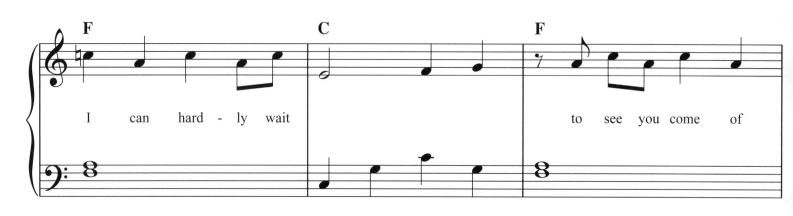

F   **C**   **F**

I can hard - ly wait   to see you come of

C   **F**   **C7**

age.   But I guess we'll   both just have to be

G7   **F**

pa - tient.   'Cause it's a   long ___ way to go,

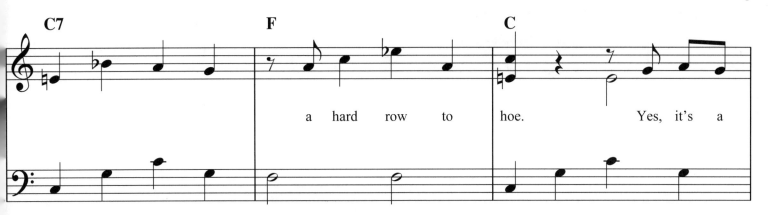

a hard row to hoe. Yes, it's a

long _____ way to go, but in the mean - time,

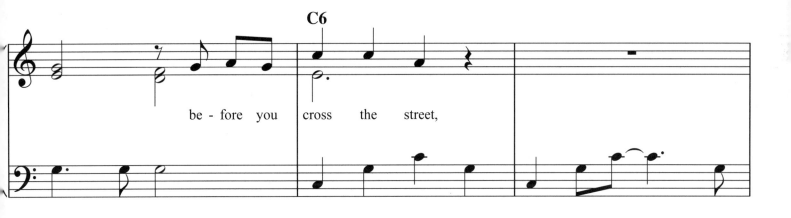

be - fore you cross the street,

take my hand. Life is what hap - pens to

6

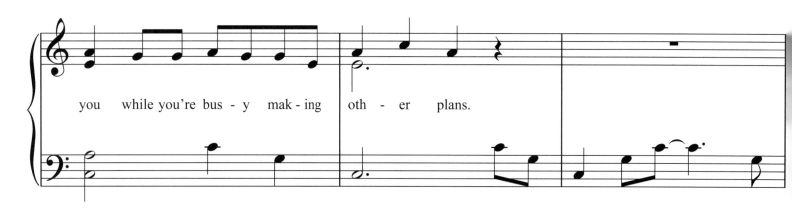

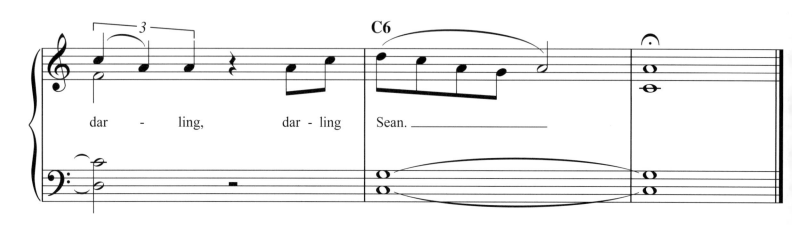

IMAGINE

Words and Music by
JOHN LENNON

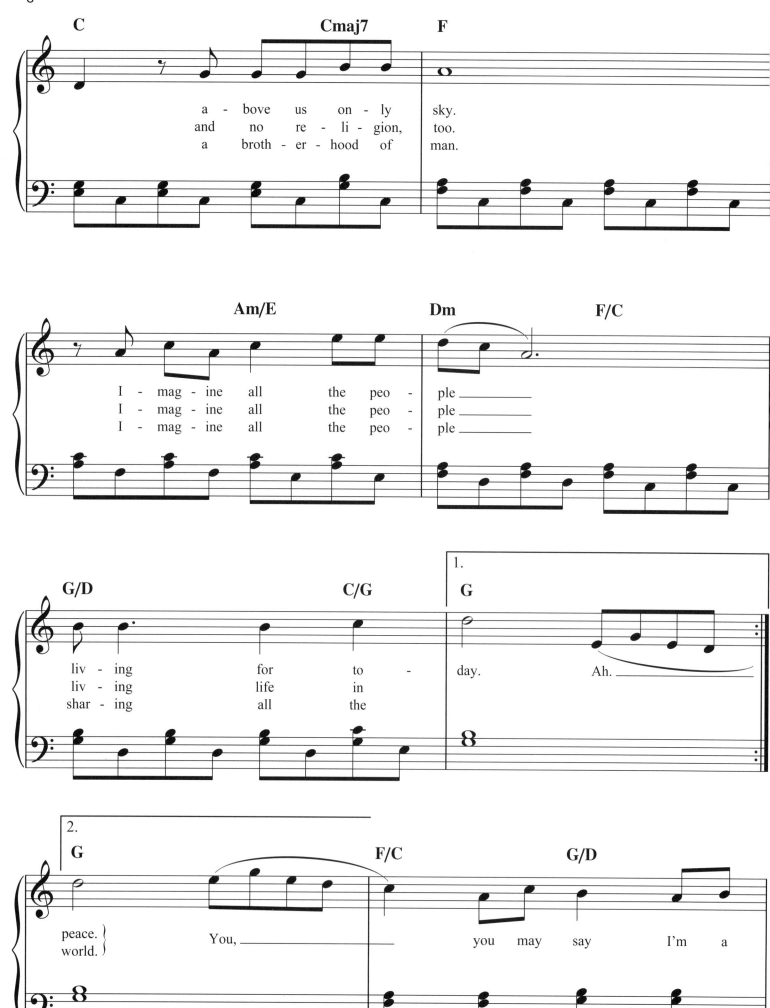

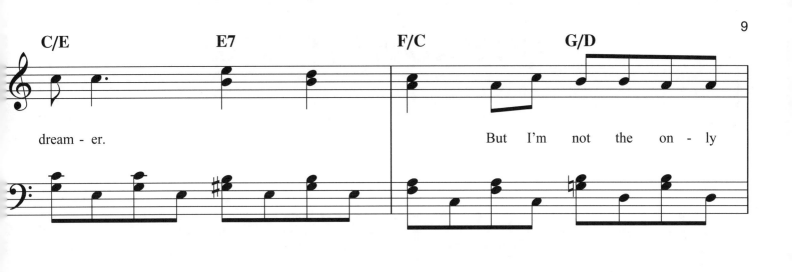

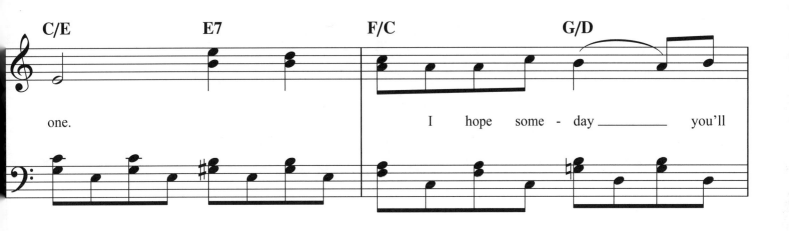

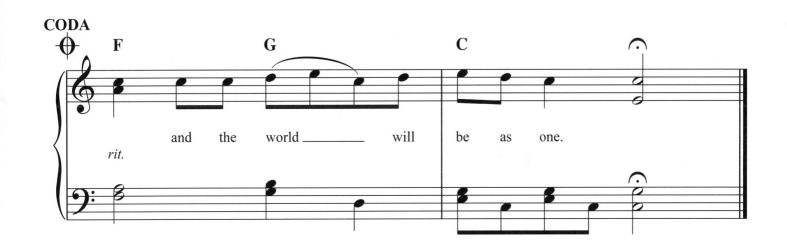

BORROWED TIME

Words and Music by
JOHN LENNON

Moderately

Lyrics under staves:

When I was young - er, _____

liv-ing con-fu - sion _____ and

deep des-pair.

When I was young-

-er _____ ah ha. _____

D

ba ba ba.

C **G**

Ba ba ba ba ___ ba ___ ba

D **D.C. al Coda** **(no repeat)** **CODA** **C**

ba ba ba.

Good to be old -

G **D** **C**

___ er, _____

{ would not ex - change __
{ less com - pli - ca -

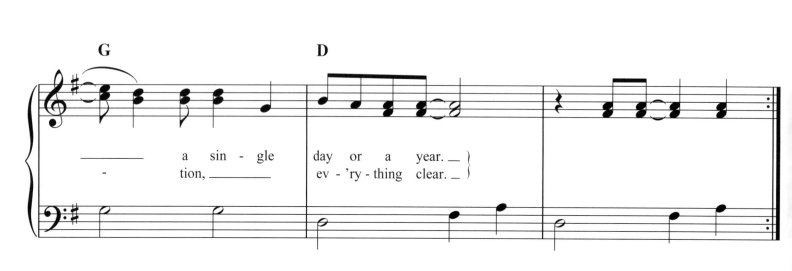

G **D**

_____ a sin - gle day or a year. _ }
\- tion, _____ ev - 'ry - thing clear. _ }

COLD TURKEY

Words and Music by
JOHN LENNON

To Coda

GIVE PEACE A CHANCE

Words and Music by
JOHN LENNON

All we ___ are say -

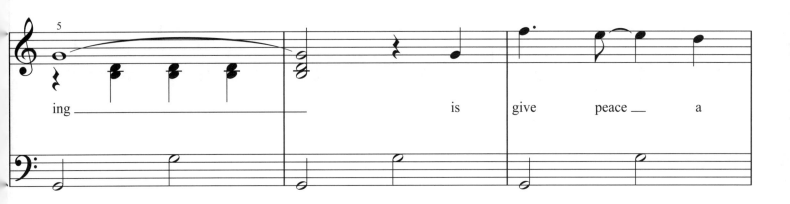

ing ___ is give peace ___ a

chance. ___

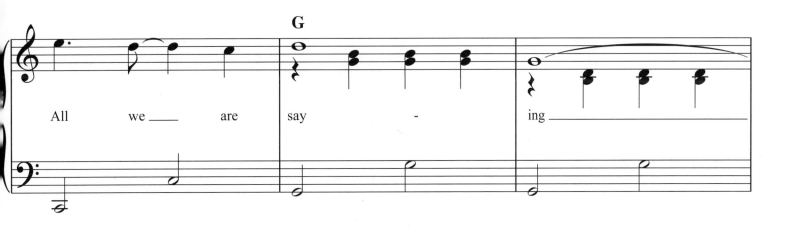

All we ___ are say - ing ___

ing _____ is

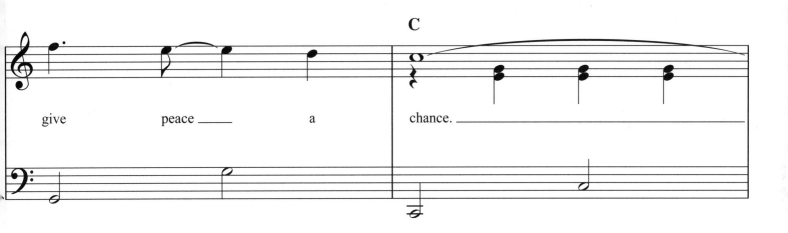

give peace ____ a chance. _____

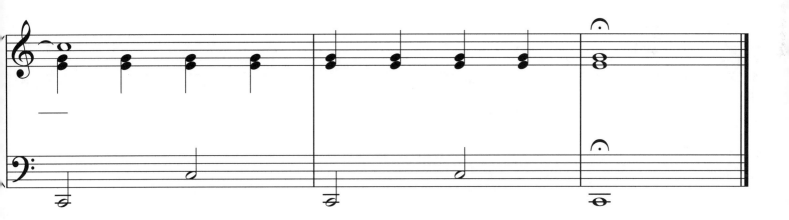

Additional Lyrics

3. Ev'rybody's talking about
   Revolution, Evolution,
   Mastication, Flagellations,
   Regulations, Integrations,
   Medication, United Nations,
   Congratulations.

4. Ev'rybody's talking about
   John and Yoko, Timmy Leary,
   Rosemary, Tommy Smothers,
   Bobby Dylan, Tommy Cooper,
   Derek Taylor, Norman Mailer,
   Allen Ginsberg, Hare Krishna
   Hare, Hare Krishna.

HAPPY XMAS
(War Is Over)

Written by JOHN LENNON
and YOKO ONO

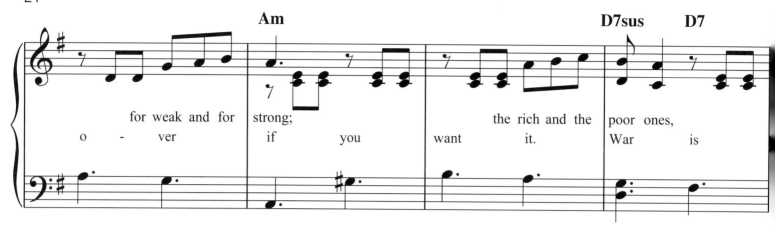

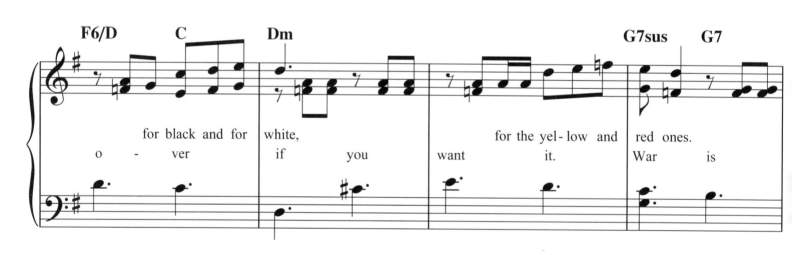

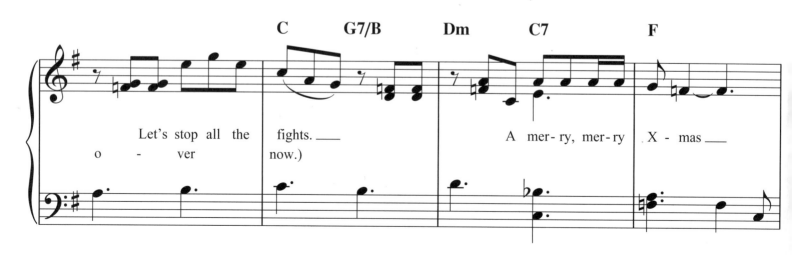

INSTANT KARMA

Words and Music by
John Lennon

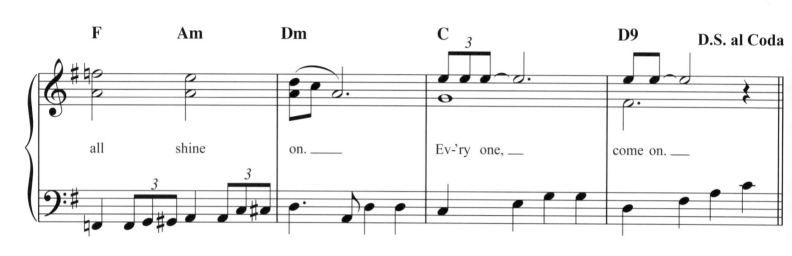

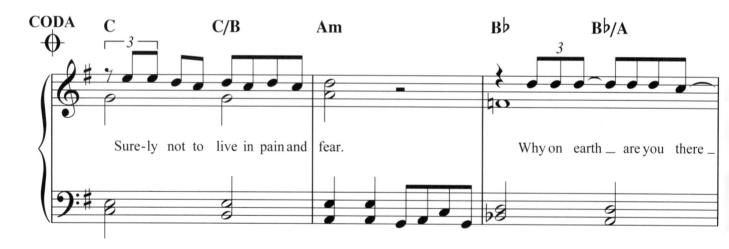

JEALOUS GUY

Words and Music by
JOHN LENNON

1. I was dream-ing of the past _____
2. I was feel-ing in - se - cure. _____
3.– 4. *(See additional lyrics)*

and my heart _____ was beat-ing fast. _____
You might not love _____ me an - y - more. _____

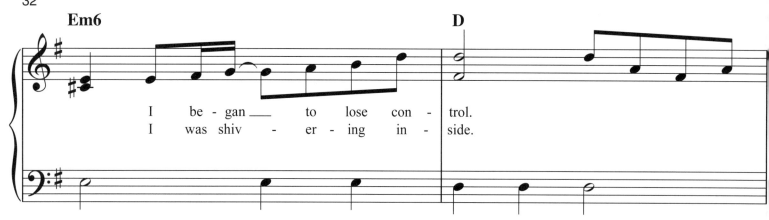

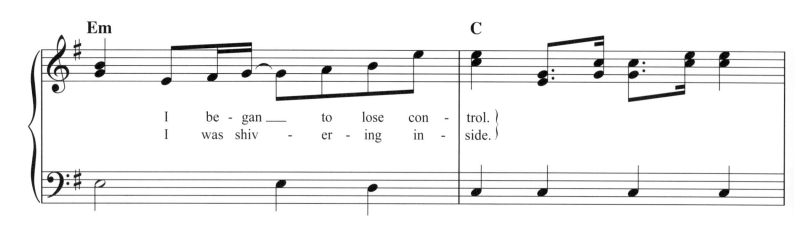

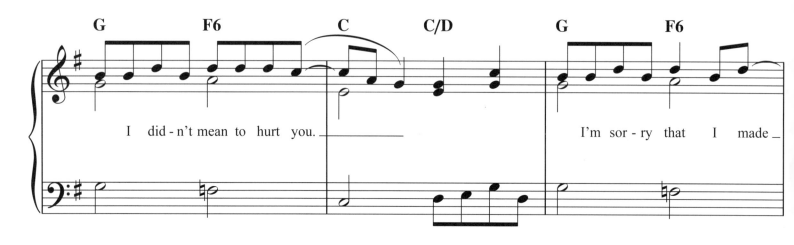

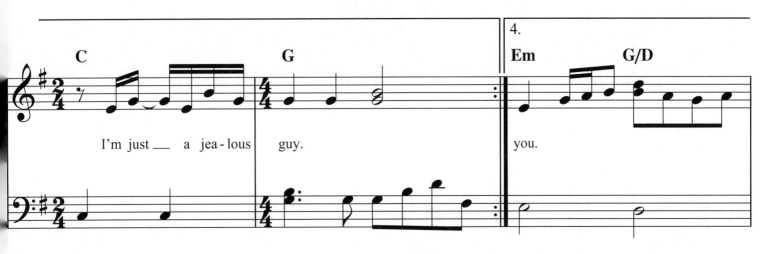

Additional Lyrics

3. Whistle.

4. I was trying to catch your eye.
   Thought that you was trying to hide.
   I was swallowing my pain.
   I was swallowing my pain.

LOVE

Words and Music by
JOHN LENNON

Love is   free, _

NOBODY TOLD ME

Words and Music by
JOHN LENNON

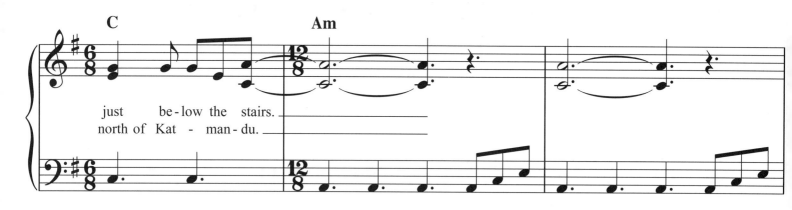

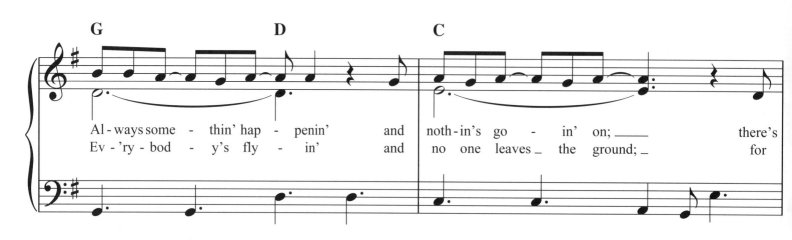

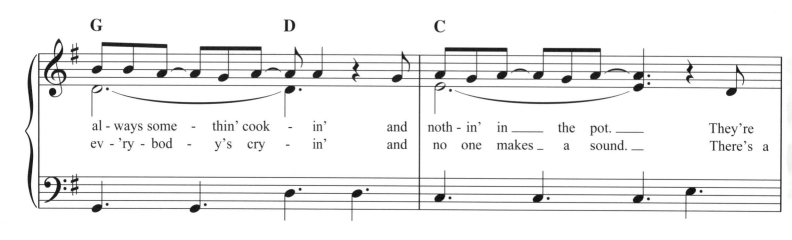

N.C.

F   C

No - bod - y told me there'd _ be days _

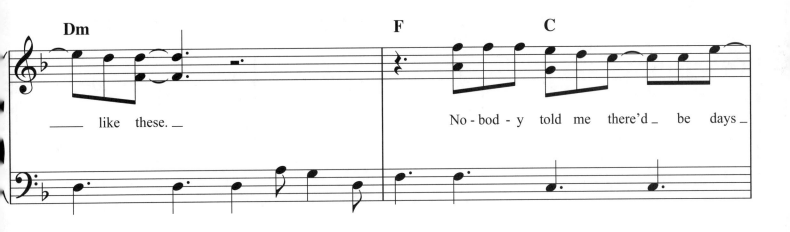

Dm

_____ like these. _

F   C

No - bod - y told me there'd _ be days _

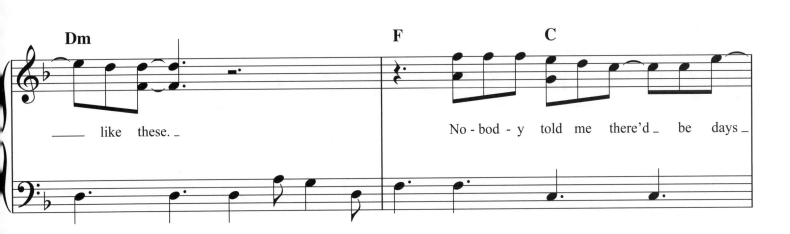

Dm

_____ like these. _

F   C

No - bod - y told me there'd _ be days _

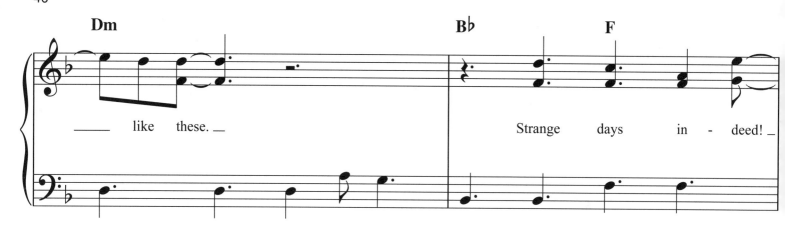

like these. ___ Strange days in - deed! _

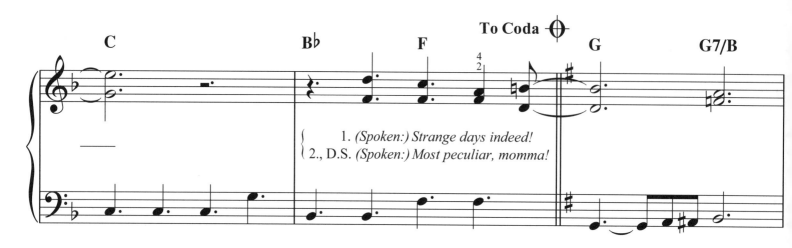

To Coda

1. (Spoken:) Strange days indeed!
2., D.S. (Spoken:) Most peculiar, momma!

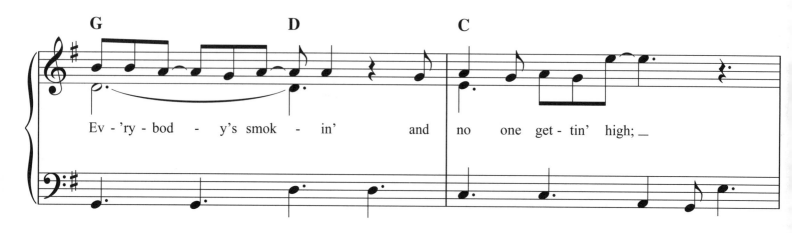

Ev - 'ry - bod - y's smok - in' and no one get - tin' high; _

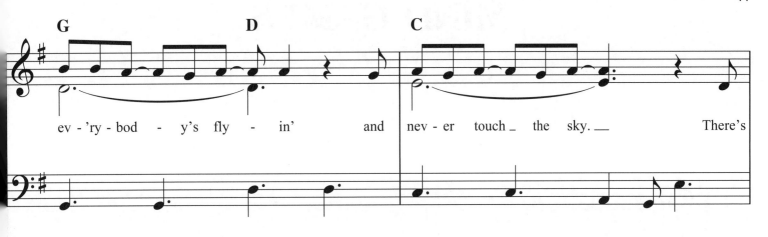

ev-'ry-bod-y's fly-in' and nev-er touch the sky. There's

D.S. al Coda

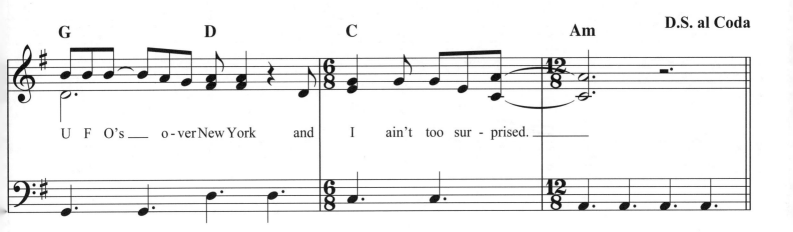

U F O's o-ver New York and I ain't too sur-prised.

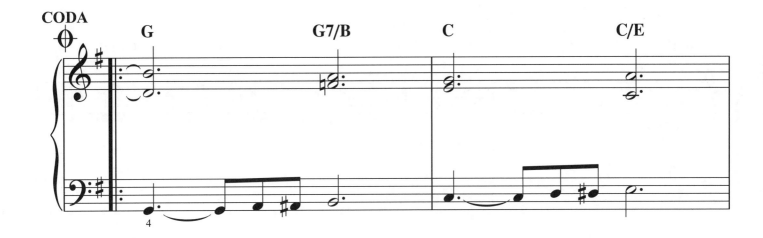

Repeat and Fade | **Optional Ending**

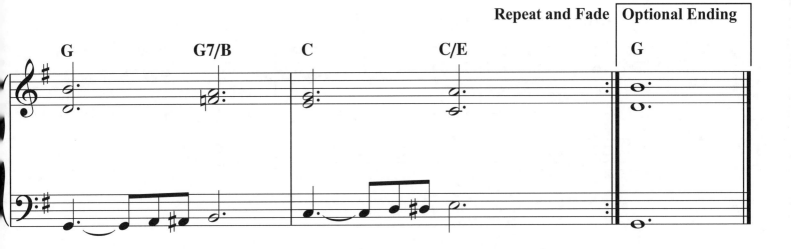

MIND GAMES

Words and Music by
JOHN LENNON

Moderately slow

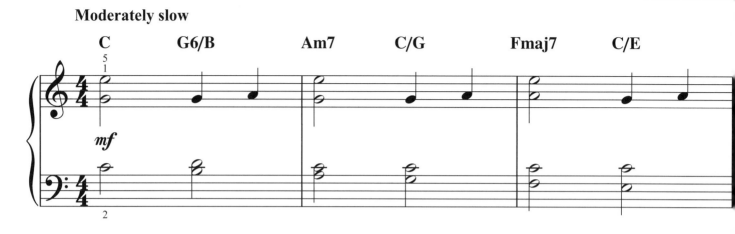

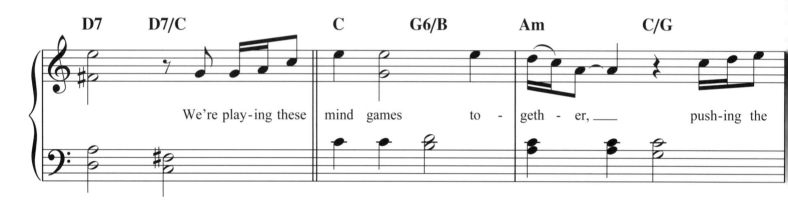

We're play-ing these mind games to - geth - er, ___ push-ing the

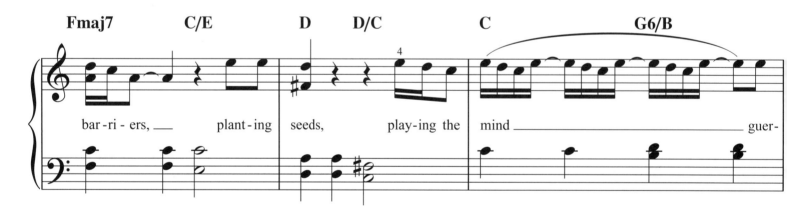

bar-ri - ers, ___ plant-ing seeds, play-ing the mind ___ guer-

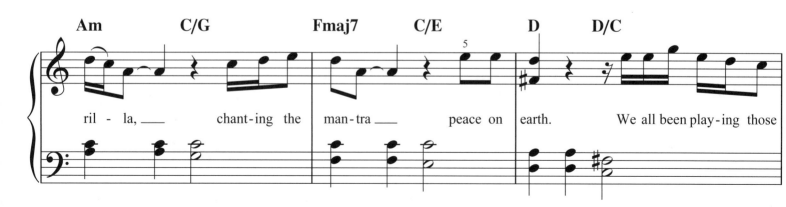

ril - la, ___ chant-ing the man-tra ___ peace on earth. We all been play-ing those

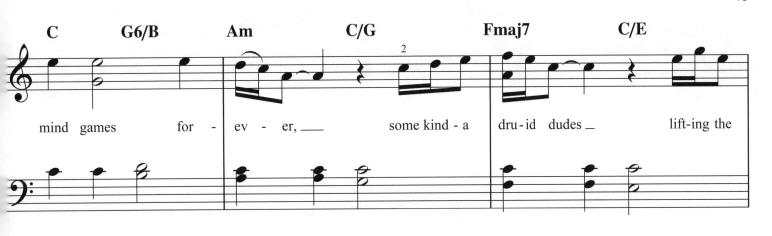

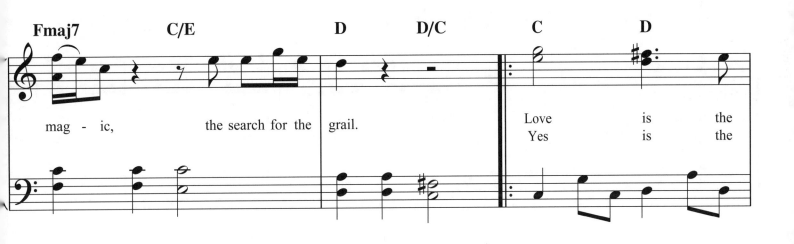

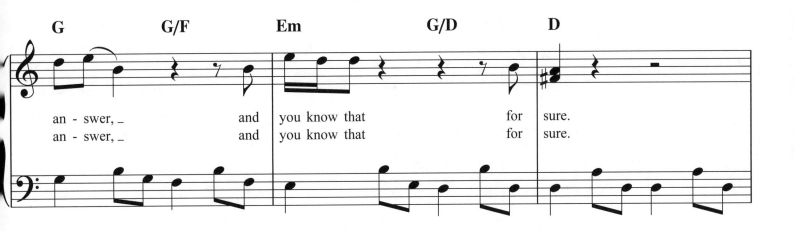

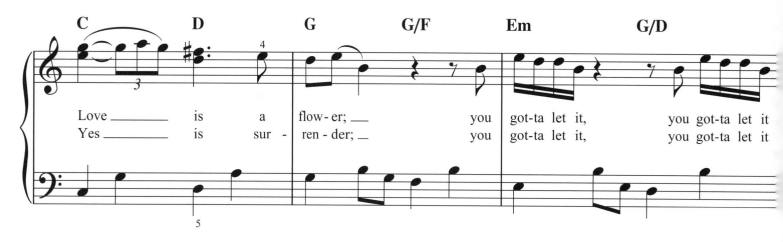

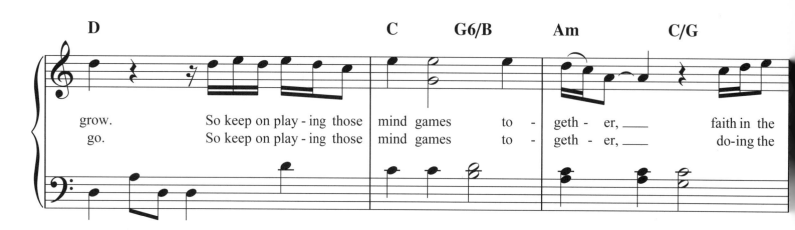

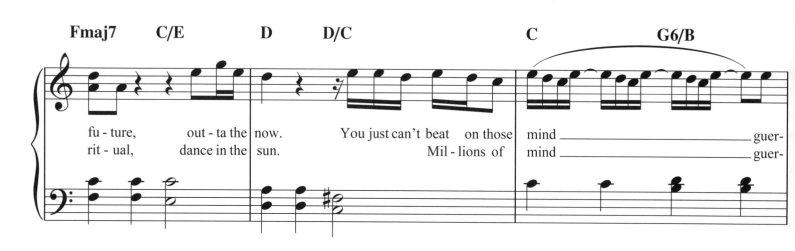

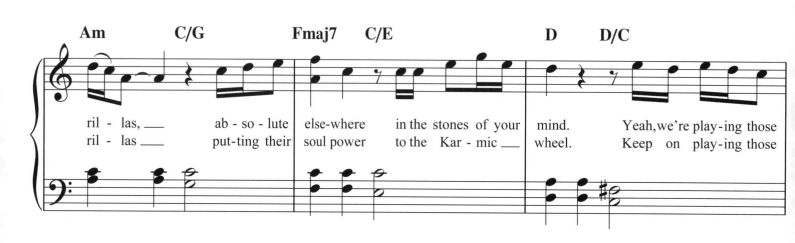

MOTHER

Words and Music by
JOHN LENNON

Slowly
Cm7/E♭

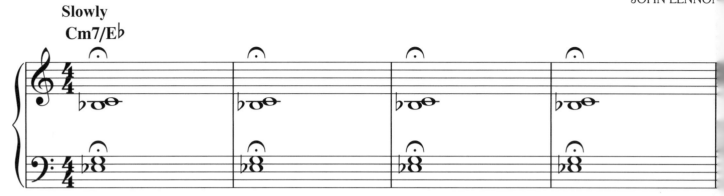

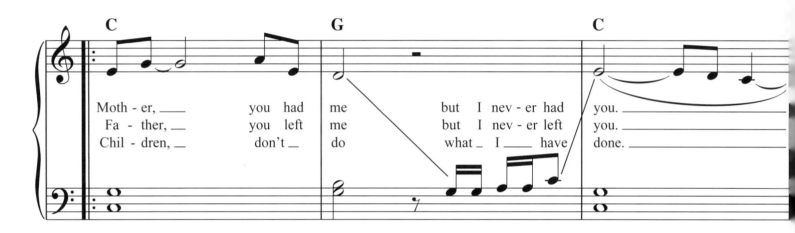

Moth - er, _____ you had me but I nev - er had you.
Fa - ther, _____ you left me but I nev - er left you.
Chil - dren, _ don't _ do what _ I _____ have done.

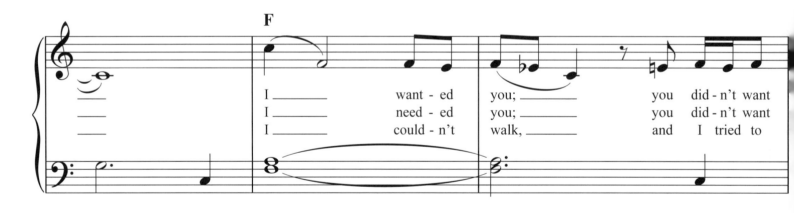

I _____ want - ed you; _____ you did - n't want
I _____ need - ed you; _____ you did - n't want
I _____ could - n't walk, _____ and I tried to

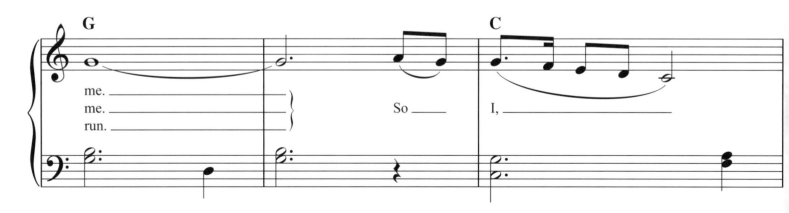

me. _____
me. _____ So _____ I, _____
run. _____

I just got to tell _____ you _____ good - bye, _____

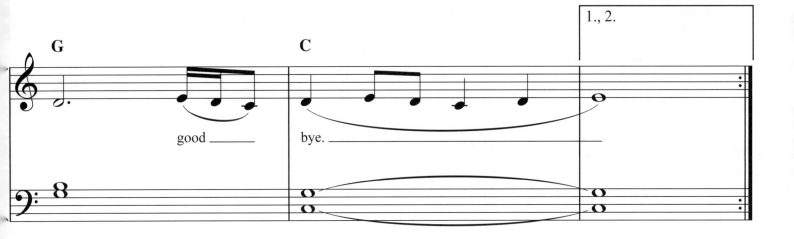

good _____ bye. _____

1., 2.

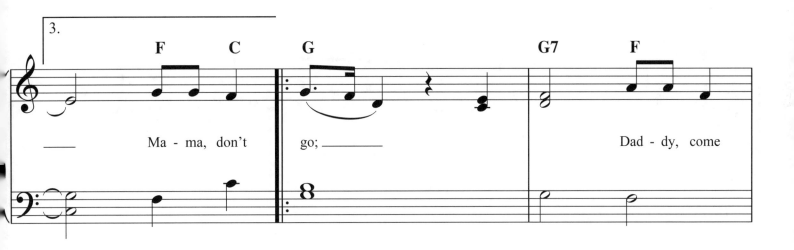

3.

_____ Ma - ma, don't go; _____ Dad - dy, come

1.

home. _____ Ma - ma, don't

2.

home. _____

#9 DREAM

Words and Music by
JOHN LENNON

Moderately

1. So _____ long a - go _____
know, _____ yes I know, _____
3., 4. *(See additional lyrics)*

through the heat whis-pered trees.

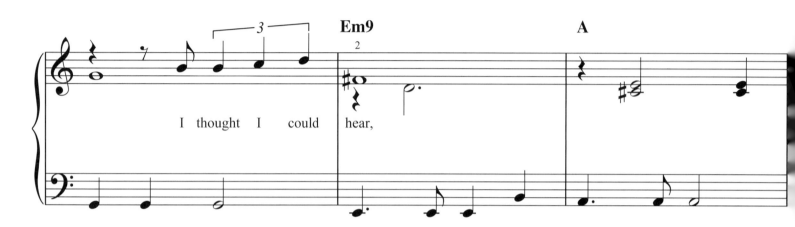

I thought I could hear,

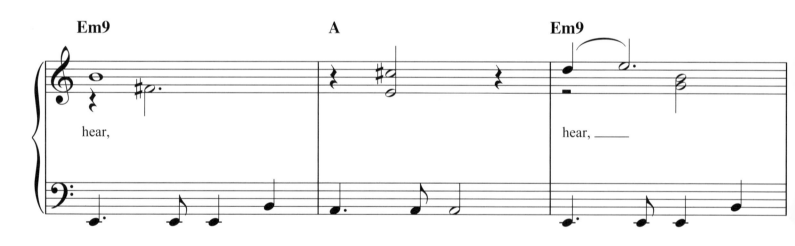

hear,

hear, ____

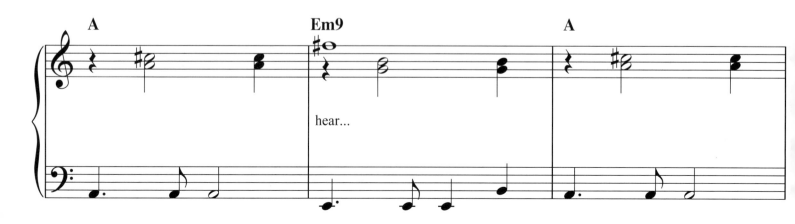

hear...

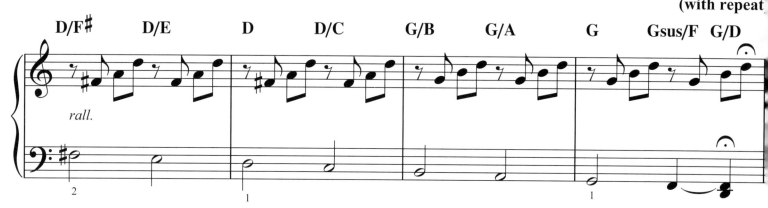

Additional Lyrics

3. Dream, dream away
   Magic in the air?
   Was magic in the air?

   On a river of sound
   Through the mirror go round, round
   I thought I could feel...
   Feel... feel... feel.

4. I believe, yes I believe
   More I cannot say
   What more can I say?

   Music touching my soul
   Something warm sudden cold
   The spirit dance was unfolding.

POWER TO THE PEOPLE

Words and Music by
JOHN LENNON

Pow - er to the peo - ple, pow - er to the peo -

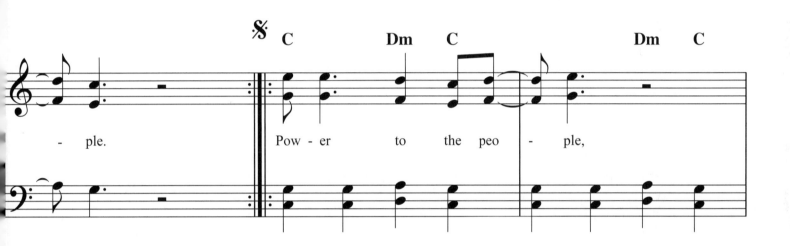

- ple. Pow - er to the peo - ple,

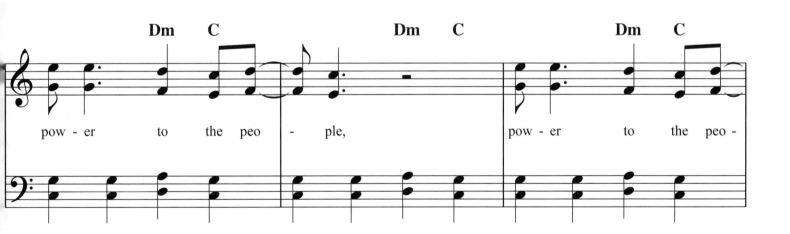

pow - er to the peo - ple, pow - er to the peo -

54

STAND BY ME

Words and Music by JERRY LEIBER
MIKE STOLLER and BEN E. KING

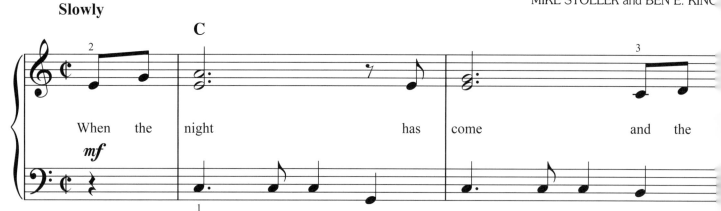

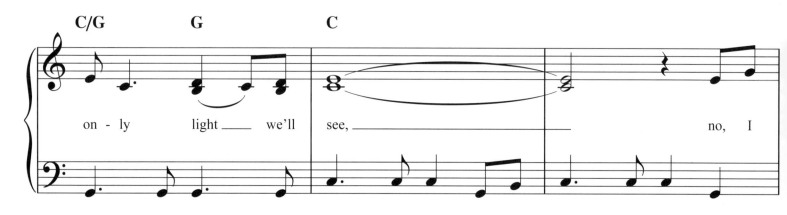

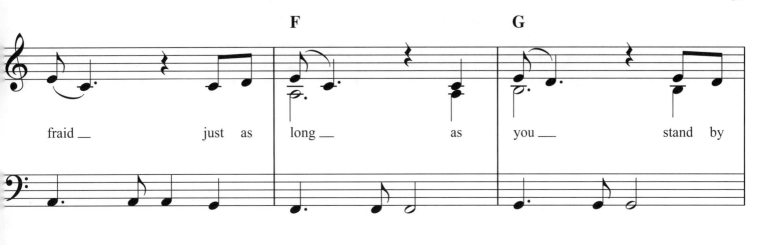

fraid ___   just as   long ___   as   you ___   stand by

me.   Dar - ling,   stand _____ by

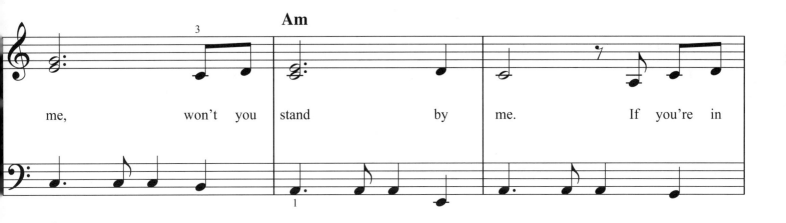

me,   won't you stand   by   me.   If you're in

need, ___   won't you   stand, ___   stand by   me.

And if the sky that we look up - on should ev - er

crum - ble and fall, and the moun - tains _____ should

fall ___ to the sea, _____ no, I

won't _ be a - fraid, _ no, I won't _____ shed a

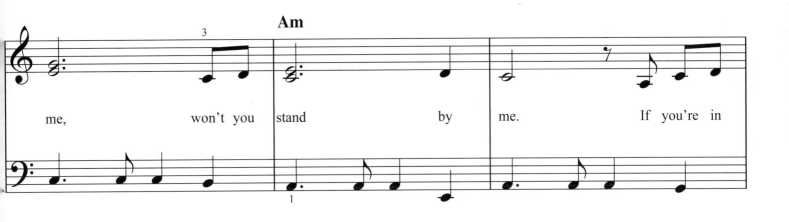

(Just Like)
STARTING OVER

Words and Music by
JOHN LENNON

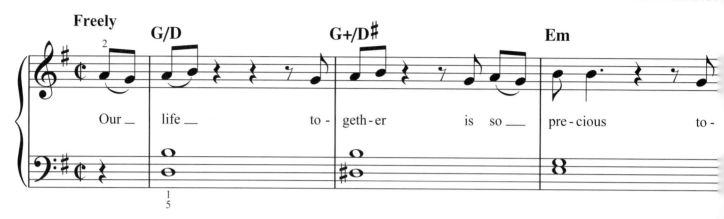

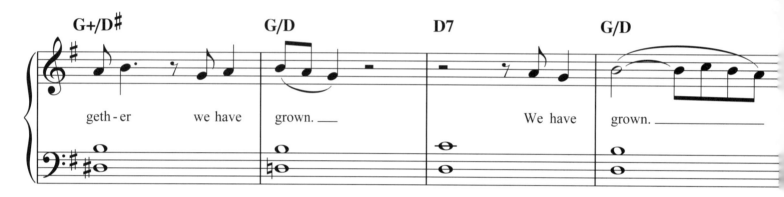

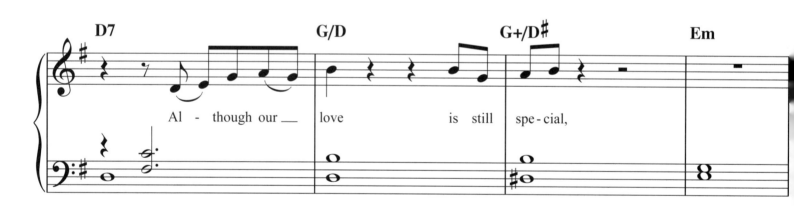

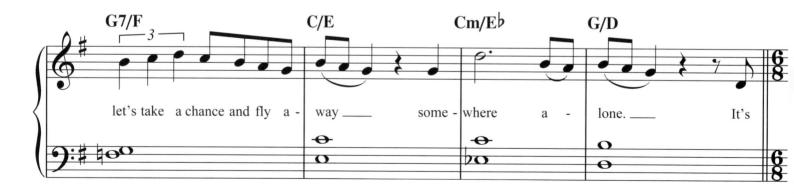

Moderately, with a strong beat

been   too   long   since   we   took   the   time. ___   No   one's   to   blame.   I
day   we   used ___   to   make   it,   love. ___   Why   can't   we   be

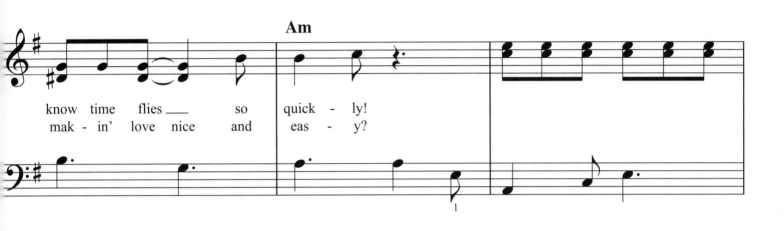

know   time   flies ___   so   quick - ly!
mak - in'   love   nice   and   eas - y?

But
It's

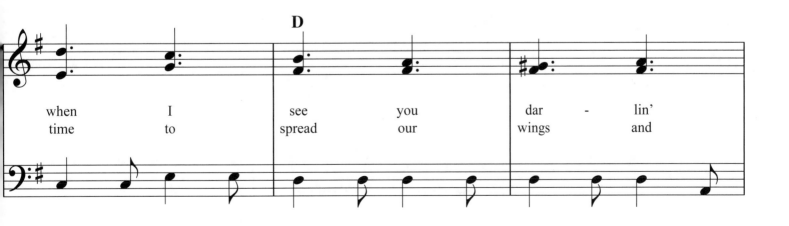

when   I   see   you   dar - lin'
time   to   spread   our   wings   and

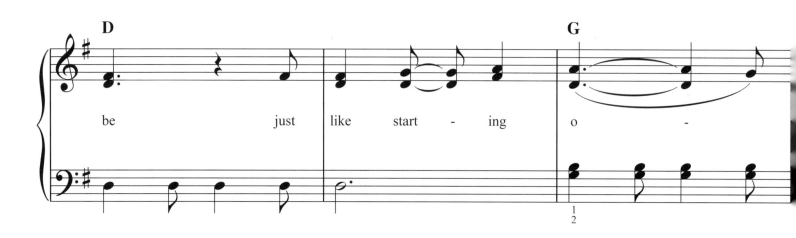

F ... **Dm**

far a - way. ___

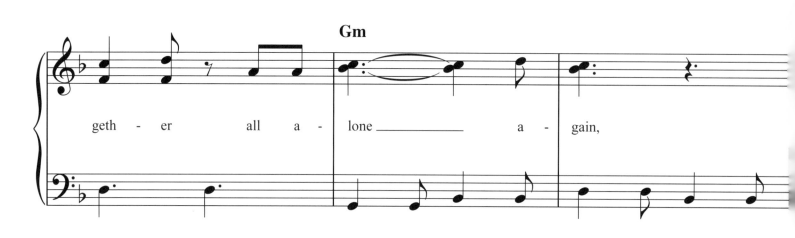

Gm

geth - er all a - lone ___ a - gain,

C7 ... **F**

like we used to ___ in the ear - ly days. ___

D.S. al Coda
(with repeat)

CODA

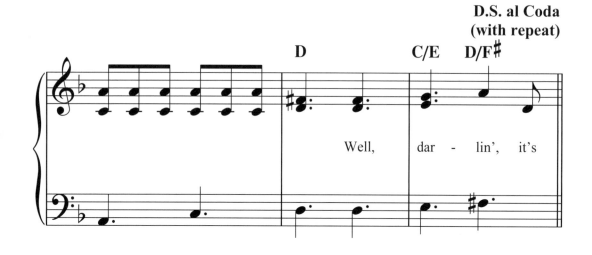

D   **C/E**   **D/F♯**

Well, dar - lin', it's

WATCHING THE WHEELS

Words and Music by
JOHN LENNON

Peo- ple say I'm cra - zy
Peo- ple say I'm laz - y,
Peo- ple ask- ing ques - tions,

do- in' what I do - in'.
dream- in' my life a - way.
lost in con- fu - sion.

Well, they give me all kinds of warn -
Well, they give me all kinds of ad -
Well, I tell them there's no prob -

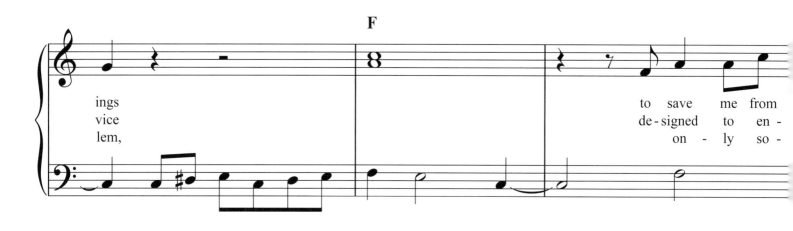

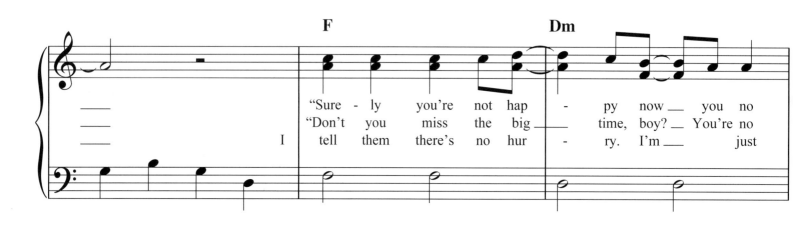

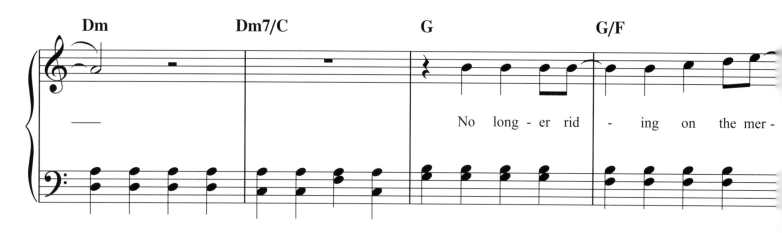

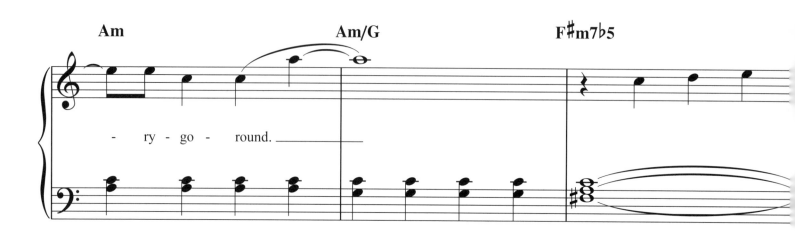

WHATEVER GETS YOU THROUGH THE NIGHT

Words and Music by
JOHN LENNON

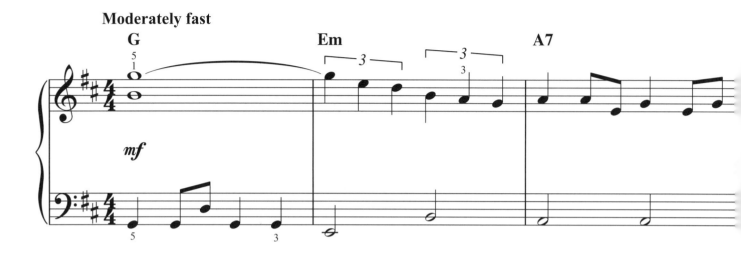

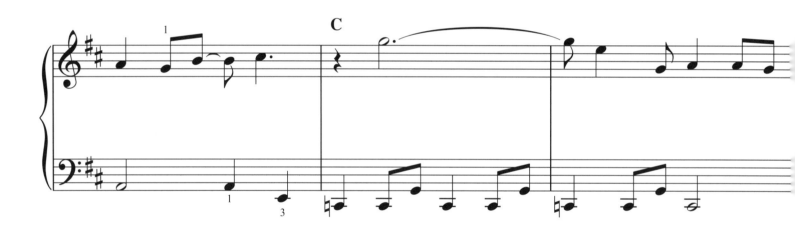

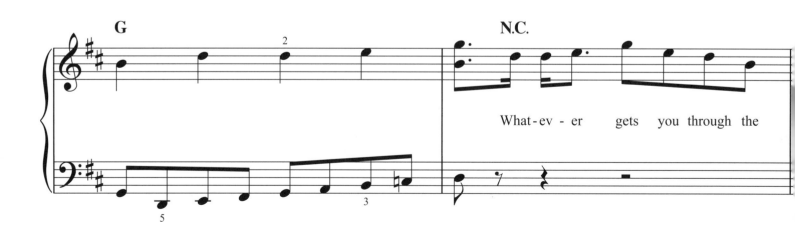

What-ev - er   gets   you through the

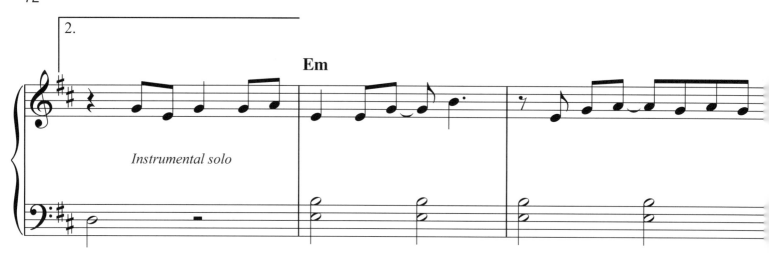

Instrumental solo

Solo ends

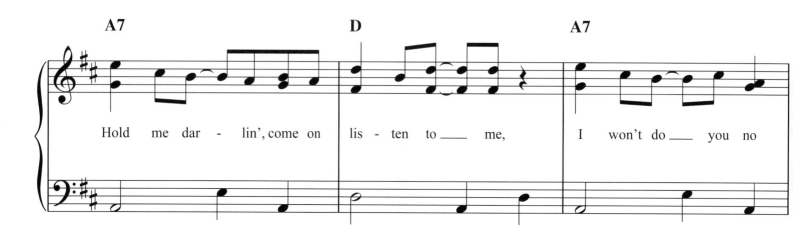

Hold me dar - lin', come on lis - ten to ___ me, I won't do ___ you no

harm;   trust me dar - lin', come on   lis - ten to ___ me, come on

lis - ten to ___ me, come on   lis - ten, lis - ten. ___   *Instrumental solo*

Solo ends   What - ev - er   gets you through the

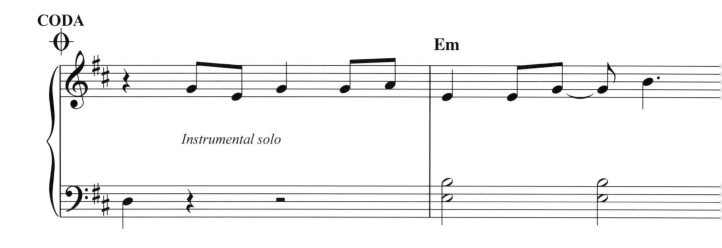

WOMAN

Words and Music
JOHN LENNO

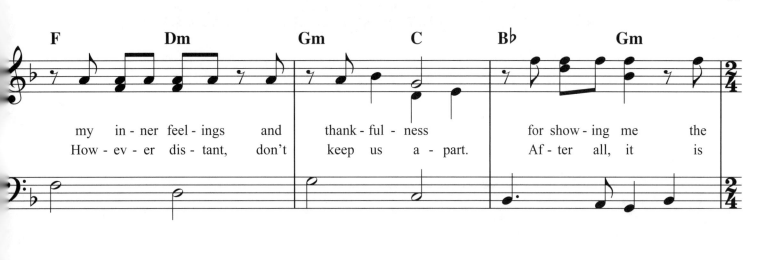

my in - ner feel - ings and | thank - ful - ness | for show - ing me the
How - ev - er dis - tant, don't | keep us a - part. | Af - ter all, it is

mean - ing of suc - | cess. _____ | I
writ - ten in the | stars. _____ |

Ooh, _____ | well, well. | Doo doo doo
love _____ you, | yeah, yeah, | now and for -

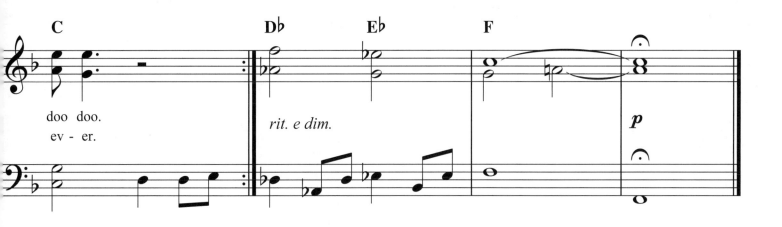

doo doo. | rit. e dim. | *p*
ev - er.

WORKING CLASS HERO

Words and Music
JOHN LENNON

pain is so big you feel noth-ing at all. ___
so fuck-ing cra-zy you can't fol-low their rules.
can't real-ly func-tion, you're so full of fear. ___

Chorus

A work-ing class he-ro is some-thing to be, ___

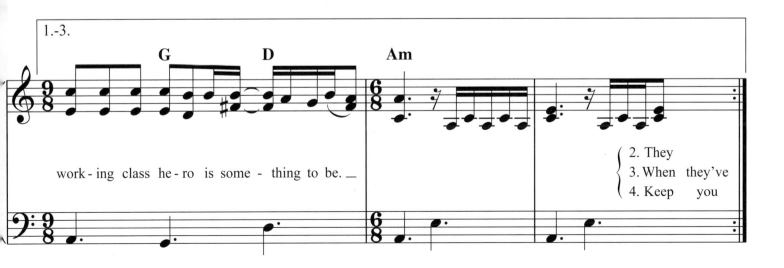

1.-3.

work-ing class he-ro is some-thing to be. __

2. They
3. When they've
4. Keep you

Additional Lyrics

4. Keep you doped with religion and sex and TV.
   And you think you're so clever and classless and free,
   But you're still fucking peasants as far as I can see.
   Chorus

5. There's room at the top they are telling you still.
   But first you must learn how to smile as you kill,
   If you want to be like the folks on the hill.
   Chorus